D1388174

First published by Brockhampton Press Ltd
20 Bloomsbury Street
London WC1B 3QA

© Brockhampton Press Ltd, 1997
© Savitri Books Ltd (illustrations and anthology), 1997

ISBN 1 86019 401 X

All rights reserved. No part of this publication may be
reproduced, stored in a retrieval system, or transmitted
in any form or by any means, electronic, mechanical,
photocopying, recording or otherwise, without the prior
permission of the copyright owners.

Conceived and designed by Savitri Books Ltd
Anthology compiled by Caroline Taggart
Printed and bound in Italy

Book of Hours

BROCKHAMPTON PRESS

DAWN

When in the east the morning ray
Hangs out the colours of the day,
The bee through these known alleys hums
Beating the dian with its drums,
Then flowers their drowsy eyelids raise,
Their silken ensigns each displays,
And dries its pan yet dank with dew,
And fills its flask with odours new.

Andrew Marvell, *The Garden of
Appleton House*

Beautiful must be the mountains whence ye
    come,
And bright in the fruitful valleys the streams,
    wherefrom
    Ye learn your song:
Where are those starry woods? O might I
    wander there,
Among the flowers, which in that heavenly air
    Bloom the year long!

Robert Bridges, *Nightingales*

*F*or winter's rains and ruins are over,
   And all the season of snows and sin;
The days dividing lover and lover,
   The light that loses, the night that wins;
And time remembered is grief forgotten,
And frosts are slain and flowers begotten,
And in green underwood and over
   Blossom by blossom the spring begins.

Algernon Swinburne, *Atalanta in Calydon*

*L*ove, whose month is ever May,
Spied a blossom passing fair,
Playing in the wanton air.

William Shakespeare,
Love's Labour's Lost

'*M*ost musical, most melancholy' bird!
A melancholy bird? Oh, idle thought!
In Nature there is nothing melancholy.

Samuel Taylor Coleridge,
The Nightingale

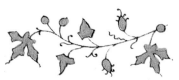

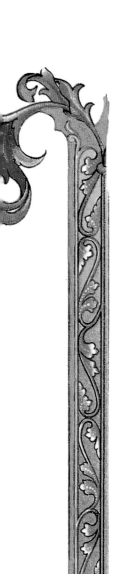

Books! 'tis a dull and endless strife:
  Come, hear the woodland linnet,
How sweet his music! on my life,
  There's more of wisdom in it.

And hark! how blithe the throstle sings!
  He, too, is no mean preacher:
Come forth into the light of things,
  Let Nature be your teacher.

William Wordsworth,
The Tables Turned

We saw thee in thy balmy nest,
  Bright dawn of our eternal day!
We saw thine eyes break from their East
  And chase the trembling shades away.
We saw thee and we blessed the sight;
We saw thee by thy own sweet light.

Richard Crashaw,
The Shepherds' Hymn

Night's candles are burnt out, and jocund day
Stands tiptoe on the misty mountain tops.

William Shakespeare, *Romeo and Juliet*

*T*hen awake! the heavens look bright, my dear;
'Tis never too late for delight, my dear;
   And the best of all ways
   To lengthen our days
Is to steal a few hours from the night, my dear!

       Thomas Moore, *Irish Melodies*

*T*he sun does arise,
And make happy the skies.
The merry bells ring
To welcome the spring.
The skylark and thrush,
The birds of the bush,
Sing louder around,
To the bells' cheerful sound,
While our sports shall be seen
On the echoing green.

       William Blake,
      The Echoing Green

*B*rightly dawns our wedding day;
Joyous hour, we give thee greeting!

     W S Gilbert, *The Mikado*

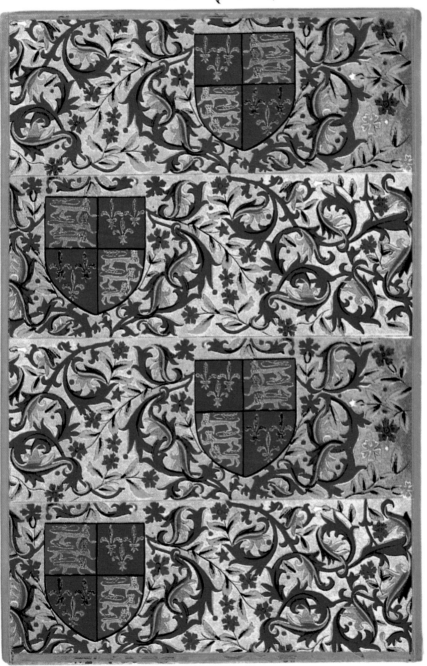

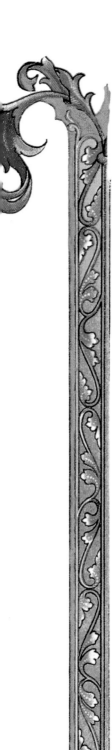

But the day when I rose at dawn from the
    bed of perfect health,
refresh'd, singing, inhaling the ripe breath
    of autumn,
When I saw the full moon in the west grow
    pale and disappear in the morning light,
When I wander'd alone over the beach,
    and undressing bathed,
laughing with the cool waters, and saw the
    sun rise,
And when I thought how my dear friend
    my lover was on his way coming,
      O then I was happy.

Walt Whitman,
When I Heard at the Close of the Day

Pray but one prayer for me 'twixt thy closed
    lips;
Think but one thought of me up in the stars.
The summer night waneth, the morning light
    slips,
Faint and grey 'twixt the leaves of the aspen,
    betwixt the cloud-bars,
That are patiently waiting there for the dawn:
Patient and colourless, though Heaven's gold
Waits to float through them along with the sun.

William Morris, *Summer Dawn*

The point of one white star is quivering still
Deep in the orange light of widening morn
Beyond the purple mountains: through a chasm
Of wind-divided mist the darker lake
Reflects it; now it wanes; it gleams again
As the waves fade, and as the burning threads
Of woven cloud unravel in pale air.

Percy Bysshe Shelley, *Prometheus Unbound*

Before the stars have left the skies,
At morning in the dark I rise;
And shivering in my nakedness,
By the cold candle bathe and dress.

Robert Louis Stevenson,
Winter Time

Awake! for Morning in the Bowl of Night
Has flung the Stone that puts the Stars to
    Flight:
    And Lo! the Hunter of the East has caught
The Sultan's Turret in a Noose of Light.

Edward Fitzgerald, *Omar Khayyam*

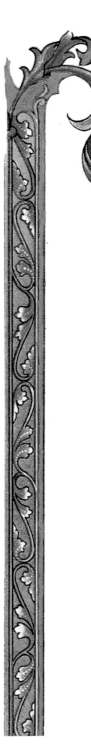

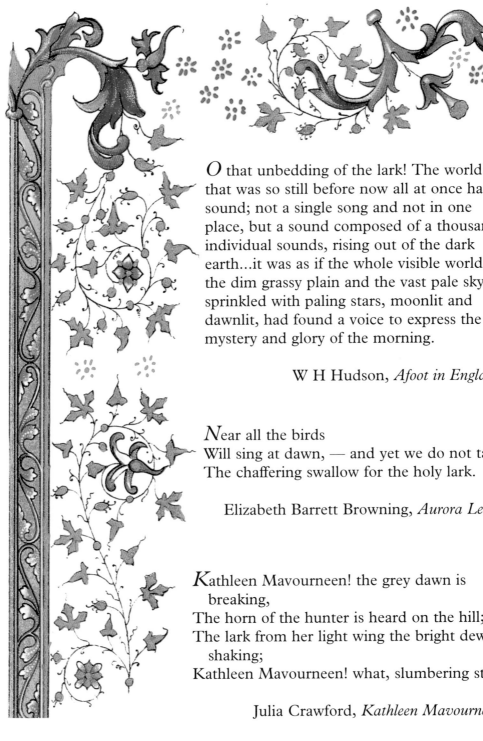

O that unbedding of the lark! The world
that was so still before now all at once had a
sound; not a single song and not in one
place, but a sound composed of a thousand
individual sounds, rising out of the dark
earth...it was as if the whole visible world,
the dim grassy plain and the vast pale sky
sprinkled with paling stars, moonlit and
dawnlit, had found a voice to express the
mystery and glory of the morning.

W H Hudson, *Afoot in England*

*N*ear all the birds
Will sing at dawn, — and yet we do not take
The chaffering swallow for the holy lark.

Elizabeth Barrett Browning, *Aurora Leigh*

*K*athleen Mavourneen! the grey dawn is
   breaking,
The horn of the hunter is heard on the hill;
The lark from her light wing the bright dew is
   shaking;
Kathleen Mavourneen! what, slumbering still?

Julia Crawford, *Kathleen Mavourneen*

Morning

Snow fallen upon the leaves had in the night
coined or morselled itself into pyramids like
hail. Blade leaves of some bulbous plant,
perhaps a small iris, were like delicate little
saws, so hagged with frost.

Gerard Manley Hopkins, *Diary*

Beautiful days, cloudless,
windless, cool in the night, warm
by day. Faintly misty. The sky pale
blue. On Wimbledon Common
every morning immense
orchestration of birds. How they
pipe and trill. A rabbit this
morning fled out of a clump of
bracken almost under my feet...
We had the place quite to ourselves
from eight until ten; just ourselves
and the birds and the rabbit.

J R Ackerley, *My Sister and Myself*

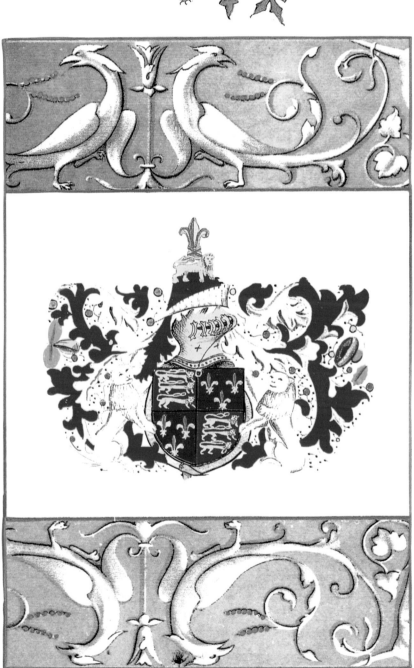

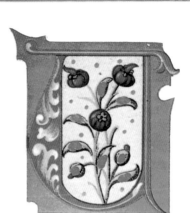

*P*ack, clouds, away, and welcome day,
With night we banish sorrow;
Sweet air blow soft, mount larks aloft
To give my Love good-morrow!

Thomas Heywood,
Pack, Clouds, Away

*B*eloved, it is morn!
A redder berry on the thorn,
A deeper yellow on the corn,
For this good day new-born;
Pray, Sweet, for me
That I may be
Faithful to God and thee.

Emily Henrietta Hickey,
Beloved, It Is Morn

*Y*ou must wake and call me early, call me
early, mother dear;
To-morrow 'ill be the happiest time of all the
glad New-year;
Of all the glad New-year, mother, the maddest,
merriest day;
For I'm to be Queen o' the May, mother, I'm
to be Queen o' the May.

Alfred, Lord Tennyson, *The May Queen*

*I*n the merry month of May,
In a morn by break of day,
Forth I walked by the wood side,
Whereas May was in his pride.

Nicholas Breton,
The Ploughman's Song

*D*rove down to Robertsbridge in the early
morning with Illingworth — glorious
morning with mist gradually clearing as we
drove along. Spirits rose as we got further
from London.

Malcolm Muggeridge, *Diaries*

*W*ho is 't now we hear?
None but the lark so shrill and clear;
How at heaven's gates she claps her wings,
The morn not waking till she sings.
Hark, hark, with what a pretty throat
Poor Robin redbreast tunes his note;
Hark how the jolly cuckoos sing
Cuckoo, to welcome in the spring,
Cuckoo, to welcome in the spring.

John Lyly, *Welcome to Spring*

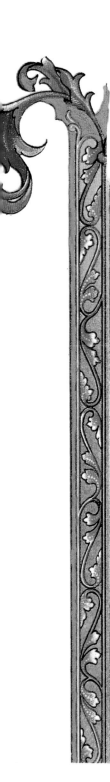

'Yes,' I answered you last night;
 'No,' this morning, sir, I say.
Colours seen by candle-light
 Will not look the same by day.

Elizabeth Barrett Browning,
The Lady's Yes

I love to rise in a summer morn,
When the birds sing on every tree;
The distant huntsman winds his horn,
And the skylark sings with me.
Ah! what sweet company.

William Blake, *The Schoolboy*

Are not the joys of morning sweeter
Than the joys of night,
And are the vig'rous joys of youth
Ashamed of the light?

Let age and sickness silent rob
The vineyards in the night,
But those who burn with vig'rous youth
Pluck fruits before the light.

William Blake, *Are Not the Joys*

*I*n the morning when I arose the mists were hanging over the opposite hills & the tops of the highest hills were covered with snow. There was a most lovely combination at the head of the vale — of the yellow autumnal hills wrapped in sunshine, & overhung with partial mists, the green & yellow trees & the distant snow-topped mountains. It was a most heavenly morning.

Dorothy Wordsworth, *Grasmere Journal*

I remember, I remember,
The house where I was born,
The little window where the sun
Came peeping in at morn.

Thomas Hood, *I Remember*

*I*t was a warm mild morning with threatenings of rain. The vale of Little Langdale looked bare & unlovely. Collath was wild & interesting, from the peat carts and peat gatherers — the valley all perfumed with the Gale & wild thyme. The woods above the waterfall veined with rich yellow broom.

Dorothy Wordsworth, *Grasmere Journal*

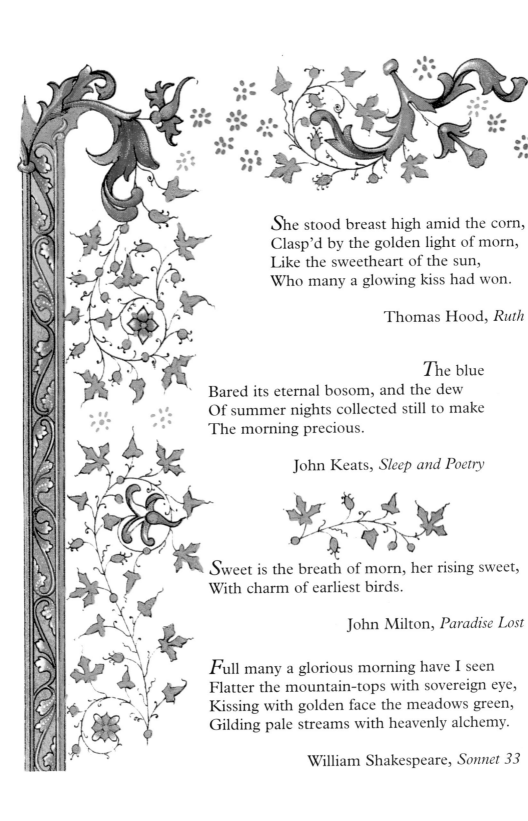

She stood breast high amid the corn,
Clasp'd by the golden light of morn,
Like the sweetheart of the sun,
Who many a glowing kiss had won.

Thomas Hood, *Ruth*

The blue
Bared its eternal bosom, and the dew
Of summer nights collected still to make
The morning precious.

John Keats, *Sleep and Poetry*

Sweet is the breath of morn, her rising sweet,
With charm of earliest birds.

John Milton, *Paradise Lost*

Full many a glorious morning have I seen
Flatter the mountain-tops with sovereign eye,
Kissing with golden face the meadows green,
Gilding pale streams with heavenly alchemy.

William Shakespeare, *Sonnet 33*

*E*arth hath not anything to show more fair:
Dull would he be of soul who could pass by
A sight so touching in its majesty:
This City now doth like a garment wear
The beauty of the morning; silent, bare
Ships, towers, domes, theatres, and temples lie
Open unto the fields, and to the sky;
All bright and glittering in the smokeless air.

William Wordsworth,
Sonnet Composed upon Westminster Bridge

*T*he year's at the spring,
And day's at the morn;
Morning's at seven;
The hill-side's dew-pearled;
The lark's on the wing;
The snail's on the thorn;
God's in his heaven —
All's right with the world!

Robert Browning,
Pippa Passes

*B*ut look, the morn, in russet mantle clad,
Walks o'er the dew of yon high eastern hill.

William Shakespeare, *Hamlet*

Noon

The vex'd elm-heads are pale with the view
Of a mastering heaven utterly blue;
Swoll'n is the wind that in argent billows
Rolls across the labouring willows;
The chestnut-fans are loosely flirting,
And bared is the aspen's silky skirting;
The sapphire pools are smit with white
And silver-shot with gusty light;
While the breeze by rank and measure
Paves the clouds on the swept azure.

Gerard Manley Hopkins,
A Windy Day in Summer

Today I am by the river below East
Peckham. I'm writing letters, roasting in the
sun, sweating, burning, turning red. The
feathers of the grass tickle me and I am
almost stupefied. Oh, how lovely it is.

Denton Welch, *Journals*

When all the birds are faint with the hot sun
And hide in cooling trees, a voice will run
From hedge to hedge about the new-mown
     mead:
That is the grasshopper's — he takes the lead
In summer luxury, — he has never done
With his delights, for when tired out with fun,
He rests at ease beneath some pleasant weed.

John Keats, *The Grasshopper and the Cricket*

The day in his hotness,
The strife with the palm;
The night in her silence,
The stars in their calm.

Matthew Arnold,
Empedocles on Etna

He that has light within his own clear breast
May sit i' the centre and enjoy bright day;
But he that hides a dark soul and foul thoughts
Benighted walks under the midday sun.

John Milton, *Comus*

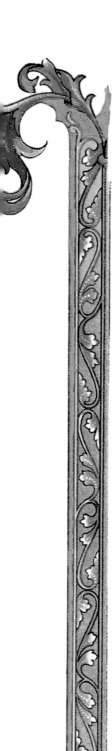

The hours I spent with thee, dear heart,
    Are as a string of pearls to me;
I count them over, every one apart,
    My rosary.

Robert Cameron Rogers, *The Rosary*

Buttercups and daisies,
Oh, the pretty flowers;
Coming ere the Springtime
To tell of sunny hours.

Mary Howitt,
Buttercup and Daisies

Being your slave, what should I do but tend
Upon the hours and times of your desire?
I have no precious time at all to spend,
Nor services to do, till you require,
Nor dare I chide the world-without-end hour
Whilst I, my sovereign, watch the clock for you.

William Shakespeare, *Sonnet 57*

*S*ee with what simplicity
This nymph begins her golden days!
   In the green grass she loves to lie,
And there with her fair aspect tames
The wilder flowers, and gives them names;
   But only with the roses plays,
         And them does tell
What colour best becomes them, and what
   smell.

Andrew Marvell,
The Picture of Little T.C.
in a Prospect of Flowers

*G*lorious day. A Plough at one end of the
field, plough man whistling melodiously. A
Harrow in another part. Sheep and lambs
dispersed about, some grazing, some at play,
others lying down. Smoke ascending from
the cottages with which the sides of the
mountain are dotted.

Lady Eleanor Butler, *Diary*

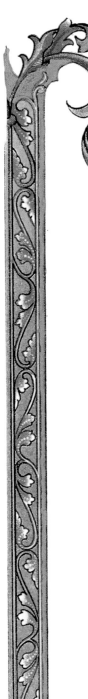

*F*air daffodils, we weep to see
  You haste away so soon;
As yet the early-rising sun
  Has not attained his noon.
    Stay, stay
  Until the hasting day
    Has run
  But to the evensong;
And, having prayed together, we
  Will go with you along.

Robert Herrick, *To Daffodils*

*A*nd what is so rare as a day in June?
  Then, if ever, come perfect days;
  Then heaven tries earth if it be in tune,
    And over it softly her warm ear lays.

James Russell Lowell,
Vision of Sir Launfal

*T*he poetry of earth is never dead:
When all the birds are faint with the hot sun,
And hide in cooling trees, a voice will run
From hedge to hedge about the new-mown
  mead.

John Keats, *The Grasshopper and the Cricket*

To the hills and the vales,
    To the rocks and the mountains,
To the musical groves
    And the cool shady fountains,
Let the triumphs of Love,
    And of Beauty be shown!
Go revel, ye Cupids,
    The day is your own!

Nahum Tate and Nicholas Brady,
                Dido and Aeneas

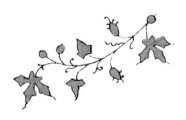

Stand still you ever-moving spheres of heaven,
That time may cease, and midnight never
    come.
Fair nature's eye, rise, rise again and make
Perpetual day, or let this hour be but
A year, a month, a week, a natural day.

Christopher Marlowe, *Faustus*

There is a land of pure delight,
Where saints immortal reign;
Infinite day excludes the night,
And pleasures banish pain.

Isaac Watts,
Hymns and Spiritual Songs

This is the last day of August and like almost
all of them of extraordinary beauty. Each day
is fine enough and hot enough for sitting out;
but also full of wandering clouds; and that
fading and rising of the light which so
enraptures me in the downs.

Virginia Woolf, *Diary*

Fly away, fly away, over the sea,
Sun-loving swallow, for summer is done.
Come again, come again, come back to me,
Bringing the summer and bringing the sun.

Christina Rossetti, *Sing-Song*

AFTERNOON

Gather ye rosebuds while ye may,
Old Time is still a-flying:
And this same flower that smiles today
To-morrow will be dying.

The glorious lamp of Heaven, the sun,
The higher he's a getting;
The sooner will his race be run,
And nearer he's to setting.

Robert Herrick, *To Virgins,*
to Make Much of Time

In the afternoon rode over to Chiddingly, to
pay my charmer, or intended wife, or
sweetheart, or whatever other name may be
more proper, a visit at her father's where I
drank tea.

Thomas Turner, *Diary*

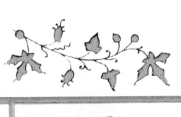
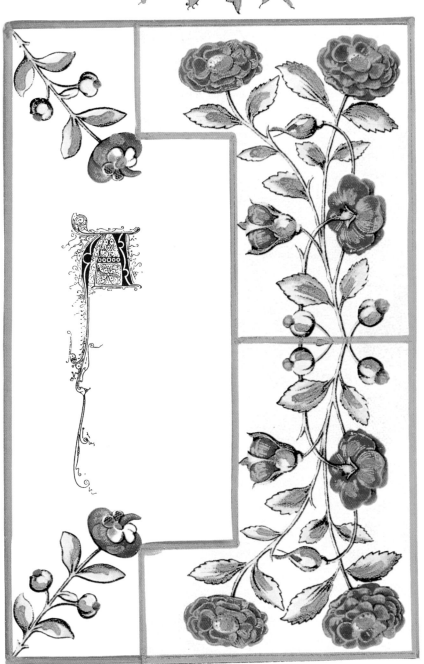

I am gone into the fields
To take what this sweet hour yields;—
Reflection, you may come tomorrow.

Percy Bysshe Shelley,
To Jane: The Invitation

*W*e reached Stourhead at 3 o'c. By that time
the sun had penetrated the mist, and was
gauzy and humid. The air about lake and
grounds of a conservatory consistency. Never
do I remember such Claude-like, idyllic
beauty here. See Stourhead and die.

James Lees-Milne, *Diary*

*T*o Oxford to see Burgo, and after lunch to
watch the Eights-week races among crowds
of variously elegant and dandified young
men, many wearing beautiful snow-white
flannels, straw hats and huge button-holes.
There was a great feeling of youth, high
spirits and promiscuous élan; also a lot of
pretty girls with peach-like complexions and
ugly clothes.

Frances Partridge, *Everything to Lose*

This is the turn of the tide. The days are lengthening. Today was fine from start to finish — the first we have had, I think, since we came. And for the first time I walked my Northease walk & saw the moon rise at 3, pale, very thin, in a pure blue sky above wide misty flattened fields, as if it were early on a June morning.

Virginia Woolf, *Diaries*

As it fell upon a day,
In the merry month of May,
Sitting in a pleasant shade,
Which a grove of myrtles made.
Beasts did leap and birds did sing,
Trees did grow and plants did spring.

Richard Barnfield,
Poems: in Divers Humours

The posterior of the day, most generous sir, is liable, congruent, and measurable, for the afternoon. The word is well cull'd, chose, sweet, and apt.

William Shakespeare, *Love's Labour's Lost*

*S*creened is this nook o'er the high, half-reaped
   field.
And here till sun-down, shepherd! will I be,
Through the thick corn, the scarlet poppies
   peep,
And round green roots and yellowing stalks
   I see
Pale pink convolvulus in tendrils creep;
And air-swept lindens yield
Their scent, and rustle down their perfumed
   showers
Of bloom on the bent grass where I am
   laid,
And bower me from the August sun with
   shade;
And the eye travels down to Oxford's towers.

Matthew Arnold, *The Scholar Gypsy*

*H*ow do I love thee? Let me count the ways.
I love thee to the depth and breadth and height
My soul can reach, when feeling out of sight
For the ends of Being and ideal Grace.
I love thee to the level of every day's
Most quiet need, by sun and candle light.

Elizabeth Barrett Browning,
Sonnets from the Portuguese

Lost, yesterday, somewhere between Sunrise
and Sunset, two golden hours, each set with
sixty diamond minutes. No reward is offered,
for they are gone forever.

Horace Mann, Lost, Two Golden Hours

Her angel's face

As the great eye of heaven shined bright,
And made a sunshine in the shady place;
Did never mortal eye behold such heavenly
   grace.

Edmund Spenser, The Faerie Queene

Deep in the sun-searched growths the
   dragon-fly
Hangs like a blue thread loosened from the
   sky:—
So this wing'd hour is dropt to us from above.
Oh! clasp we to our hearts, for deathless dower,
This close-companioned inarticulate hour
When twofold silence was the song of love.

Dante Gabriel Rossetti, The House of Life

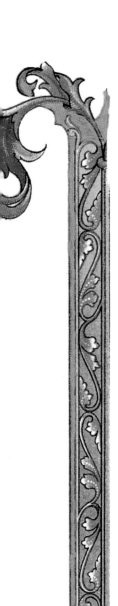

*G*o not, happy day,
From the shining fields,
Go not, happy day,
Till the maiden yields.
Rosy is the West,
Rosy is the South,
Roses are her cheeks,
And a rose her mouth.

Alfred, Lord Tennyson,
Maud

We had tea from bright blue cups under the
pink light of the giant hollyhock. We were all
a little drugged with the country; a little
bucolic, I thought. It was lovely enough —
made me envious of its country peace.

Virginia Woolf, *Diaries*

*A*nd so, from hour to hour, we ripe and ripe,
And then from hour to hour, we rot and rot:
And thereby hangs a tale.

William Shakespeare, *As You Like It*

*H*ow pleasant it is — to get into a small car
and drive away from London on a fine
Saturday afternoon. As one gets nearer open
country, one slows down to watch half a
minute of local cricket. By the time the
bowler has started to deliver his next ball one
is out of sight.

Siegfried Sassoon, *Diaries*

*T*he day becomes more solemn and serene
When noon is past — there is a harmony
In autumn and a lustre in the sky,
Which through the summer is not heard or
    seen,
As if it could not be, as if it had not been!

Percy Bysshe Shelley,
Hymn to Intellectual Beauty

*T*he meanest flowret of the vale,
The simplest note that swells the gale,
The common sun, the air, the skies,
To him are opening paradise.

Thomas Gray,
*Ode on the Pleasure Arising
from Vicissitude*

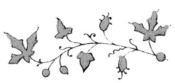

*O*r to some coffee house I stray,
For news, the manna of a day,
And from the hipp'd discourses gather
That politics go by the weather.

Matthew Green, *The Spleen*

I drew my bride, beneath the moon,
Across my threshold; happy hour!
But ah, the walk that afternoon
We saw the water-flags in flower!

Coventry Patmore,
The Angel in the House

A day in such serene enjoyment spent
Were worth an age of splendid discontent.

James Montgomery, *Greenland*

I turn to thee as some green afternoon
Turns toward sunset, and is loth to die;
Ah God, ah God, that day should be so soon!

Algernon Swinburne, *In the Orchard*

EVENING

This evening being May Eve I ought to have put some birch and wittan (mountain ash) over the door to keep out the 'old witch'. But I was too lazy to go out and get it. Let us hope the old witch will not come during the night. The young witches are welcome.

Reverend Francis Kilvert, *Diary*

The heaven being spread with this pallid screen and the earth with the darkest vegetation, their meeting-line at the horizon was clearly marked. In such contrast the heath wore the appearance of an instalment of night which had taken up its place before its astronomical hour was come: darkness had to a great extent arrived hereon, while day stood distinct in the sky.

Thomas Hardy, *Return of the Native*

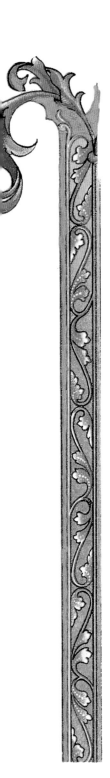

*W*hen I sit by myself at the close of the day,
And watch the blue twilight turn amber and
    grey,
With fancies as twinkling and vague as the
    stars,
And as distant as they from this life's petty
    jars —
I know not, I think not where fortune may be,
But I feel I am in very good company.

Trad, *Good Company*

*A*ve Maria! 'tis the hour of prayer!
Ave Maria! 'tis the hour of love!

George Gordon, Lord Byron,
Don Juan

*W*hile now the bright-haired sun
Sits in yon western tent, whose cloudy skirts
  With brede ethereal wove,
  O'erhang his wavy bed.

William Collins, *Ode to Evening*

The day is past, the sun is set,
   And the white stars are in the sky;
While the long grass with dew is wet,
   And through the air the bats now fly.

The lambs have now lain down to sleep,
   The birds have long since sought their nests;
The air is still; and dark, and deep
   On the hill side the old wood rests.

Thomas Miller, *Evening*

And every eve I say,
Noting my step of bliss,
That I have known no day
In all my life like this.

Robert Bridges,
The Idle Life I Lead

It was a gentle day, & when Wm & I returned
home just before sunset, it was a heavenly
evening. A soft sky was among the hills, & a
summer sunshine above, & blending with this
sky, for it was more like sky than clouds.

Dorothy Wordsworth, *Grasmere Journal*

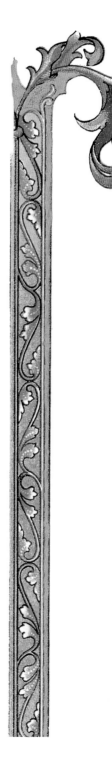

The western sun withdraws the shortened day,
And humid evening, gliding o'er the sky
In her chill progress, to the ground condensed
The vapours throws.

James Thomson, *The Autumnal Moon*

The sheep-bell tolleth curfew time;
    The gnats, a busy rout,
Fleck the warm air; the dismal owl
    Shouteth a sleepy shout;
The voiceless bat, more felt than seen,
    Is flitting round about.

The aspen leaflets scarcely stir;
    The river seem to think;
Athwart the dusk, broad primroses
    Look coldly from the brink,
Where, listening to the freshet's noise,
    The quiet cattle drink.

The bees boom past; the white moths rise
    Like spirits from the ground;
The gray flies hum their weary tune,
    A distant, dream-like sound;
And far, far off, to the slumb'rous eve,
    Bayeth an old guard-hound.

Coventry Patmore, *An Evening Scene*

*B*ut gi'e me a canny hour at e'en,
My arms about my dearie O;
An' warly cares, an' warly men,
May a' gae tapsalteerie O!

Robert Burns,
Green Grow the Rushes

*T*he sun descending in the west,
The evening star does shine.
The birds are silent in their nest,
And I must seek for mine.
The moon, like a flower
In heaven's high bower,
With silent delight
Sits and smiles on the night.

William Blake, *Night*

*A*bide with me; fast falls the eventide;
The darkness deepens; Lord, with me abide;
When other helpers fail, and comforts flee,
Help of the helpless, O, abide with me.

Henry Francis Lyte,
Remains, Abide with Me

The night is darkening round me,
The wild winds coldly blow;
But a tyrant spell has bound me
And I cannot, cannot go.

The giant trees are bending
Their bare boughs weighed with snow.
And the storm is fast descending,
And yet I cannot go.

Clouds beyond clouds above me,
Wastes beyond wastes below;
But nothing drear can move me;
I will not, cannot go.

Emily Brontë, *Spellbound*

Now came still evening on, and twilight grey
Had in her sober livery all things clad;
Silence accompanied, for beast and bird,
They to their grassy couch, these to their nests
Were slunk, all but the wakeful nightingale;
She all night long her amorous descant sung;
Silence was pleased.

John Milton, *Paradise Lost*

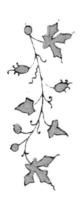

Now the day is over,
  Night is drawing nigh
Shadows of the evening
  Steal across the sky.

Now the darkness gathers,
  Stars begin to peep,
Birds and beasts and flowers
  Soon will be asleep.

Sabine Baring-Gould,
Now the Day Is Over

The curfew tolls the knell of parting day,
  The lowing herd wind slowly o'er the lea,
The ploughman homeward plods his weary
    way,
  And leaves the world to darkness and to me.

Now fades the glimmering landscape on the
    sight,
  And all the air a solemn stillness holds,
Save where the beetle wheels his droning flight,
  And drowsy tinklings lull the distant folds.

Thomas Gray,
Elegy Written in a Country Churchyard

NIGHT

When the blazing sun is gone,
When he nothing shines upon,
Then you show your little light,
Twinkle, twinkle, all the night...

In the dark blue sky you keep,
And often through my curtains peep,
For you never shut your eye,
Till the sun is in the sky.

Jane Taylor, *The Star*

It is the harvest moon! On guilded vanes
And roofs of villages, on woodland crests
And their aerial neighbourhood of nests
Deserted, on the curtained window-panes
Of rooms where children sleep, on country
  lanes
And harvest fields, its mystic splendour rests!

Henry Wadsworth Longfellow,
The Harvest Moon

Whenever the moon and stars are set,
  Whenever the wind is high,
All night long in the dark and wet,
  A man goes riding by.
Late in the night when the fires are out,
Why does he gallop and gallop about?

Robert Louis Stevenson, *Windy Nights*

    All night have the roses heard
      The flute, violin, bassoon;
      All night has the casement jessamine stirr'd
      To the dancers dancing in tune;
    'Till a silence fell with the waking bird
      And a hush with the setting moon.

        Alfred, Lord Tennyson, *Maud*

It was a fine still night, without a cloud in
the pale, dusty blue sky, thinly sprinkled with
stars, and the crescent moon coming up
above the horizon. After the cock ceased
crowing a tawny owl began to hoot, and the
long tremulous mellow sound followed me
for some distance from the village, and then
there was perfect silence.

      W H Hudson, *Afoot in England*

I arise from dreams of thee
In the first sweet sleep of night.
When the winds are breathing low,
And the stars are shining bright:
I arise from dreams of thee,
And a spirit in my feet
Hath led me — who knows how?
To thy chamber window, Sweet!

Percy Bysshe Shelley,
The Indian Serenade

*O*ft, in the stilly night,
    Ere slumber's chain has bound me,
Fond Memory brings the light
    Of other days around me.

Thomas Moore, *The Light of Other Days*

*J*ust before the clock struck twelve they
lighted their lanterns and started. The moon,
in her third quarter, had risen since the
snowstorm; but the dense accumulation of
snow-cloud weakened her power to a faint
twilight which was rather pervasive of the
landscape than traceable to the sky.

Thomas Hardy, *Under the Greenwood Tree*

Swiftly walk over the western wave,
　　Spirit of Night!
Out of the misty eastern cave,
Where, all the long and lone daylight,
Thou wovest dreams of joy and fear,
Which make thee terrible and dear —
　　Swift by thy flight!

　　　　Percy Bysshe Shelley, *To Night*

So, we'll go no more a-roving
　　So late into the night,
Though the heart be still as loving,
　　And the moon be still as bright.

For the sword outwears its sheath,
　　And the soul wears out the breast,
And the heart must pause to breathe,
　　And love itself have rest.

Though the night was made for loving,
　　And the day returns too soon,
Yet we'll go no more a-roving
　　By the light of the moon.

　　　　George Gordon, Lord Byron,
　　　　So, we'll go no more a-roving

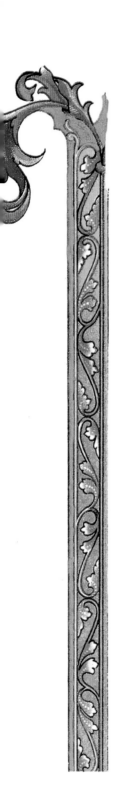

The mist that drifts away at dawn, leaving but dew in the fields, shall rise and gather into a cloud and then fall down in rain.

And not unlike the mist have I been.

In the stillness of the night I have walked in your streets, and my spirit has entered your houses.

And your heart-beats were in my heart, and your breath was upon my face, and I knew you all.

Kahlil Gibran, *The Prophet*

At the mid hour of night, when stars are
   weeping, I fly
To the lone vale we loved, when life shone
   warm in thine eye;
And I think that, if spirits can steal from the
   regions of air
To revisit past scenes of delight, thou wilt come
   to me there,
And tell me our love is remembered even in the
   sky.

Thomas Moore, *At the Mid Hour of Night*

The Frost performs its secret ministry,
Unhelped by any wind. The owlet's cry
Came loud — and hark, again! loud as
   before....
'Tis calm indeed! so calm, that it disturbs
And vexes meditation with its strange
And extreme silentness.

Samuel Taylor Coleridge, *Frost at Midnight*

But we, like sentries, are obliged to stand
In starless nights, and wait the 'pointed hour.

John Dryden, *Don Sebastian*

Something drove rattling against the
window-panes, like a handful of rain. The
moon's light had gone, and now she saw how
the dark clouds smoked across the stars.
Against them, suddenly, light beat redly, and
was gone. Then she smelt the faint, familiar
reek, and knew the clouds, the sleet, for what
they were: the ash-cone to the north, the
little Loma, had woken again and was
throwing out more ash and cinders. And the
wind blew from there.

Mary Stewart, *The Wind off the Small Isles*

In the staring darkness
I can hear the harshness
Of the cold wind blowing.
I am warmly clad,
And I'm very glad
That I've got a home.

Gerard Manley Hopkins,
In the Staring Darkness

The ledge I found for the night was sheltered
by trees on three sides and, on the fourth, the
tips of the pine trees zoomed into the depths.
When the afterglow following a bonfire-
sunset had gone and the bedtime
pandemonium of birds began to quieten, I
rugged up, lit a candle, fished out my book
and for a few pages followed the adventures
of Theodore Gumbril. The stars were
unbelievably dense, to gaze up turned one
into a multi-millionaire.

Patrick Leigh Fermor,
Between the Woods and the Water

What sweet-breathing presence
Out-perfumes the thyme?
What voices enrapture
The night's balmy prime?

Matthew Arnold,
The Song of Callicles

Look at the stars! look, look up at the skies!
O look at all the fire-folk sitting in the air!
The bright boroughs, the circle-citadels there!
Down in dim woods the diamond delves! they
   elves'-eyes!
The grey lawns cold where gold, where
   quickgold lies!
Wind-beat whitebeam! airy abeles set on a flare!
Flake-doves sent floating forth at a farmyard
   scare!—
Ah well! it is all a purchase, all is a prize.

Gerard Manley Hopkins, *The Starlight Night*

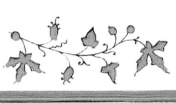
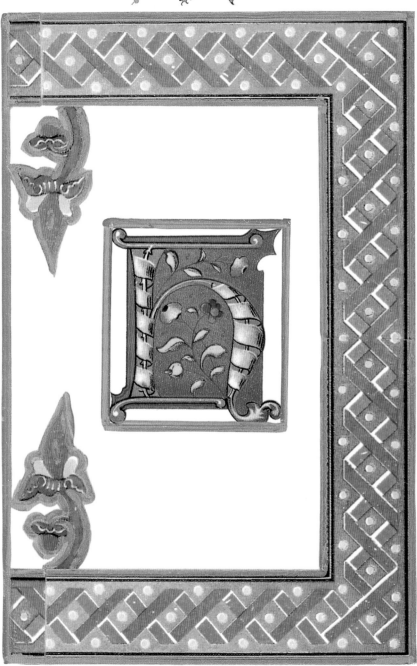